PATIO OF JAMES N. CLAPP HOUSE PASADENA

WINCHTON L. RISLEY ARCHITECT

RESIDENTIAL ARCHITECTURE IN SOUTHERN CALIFORNIA 1939

MEDITERRANEAN TO MODERN

Edited by Paul Robinson Hunter
and Walter L. Reichardt

Southern California Chapter

The American Institute
of Architects

HENNESSEY+INGALLS
Art + Architecture Books Santa Monica 1998

Originally published by the Southern California Chapter,
The American Institute of Architects, 1939.
Edited by Paul Robinson Hunter and Walter L. Reichardt.

Manufactured in the United States of America.

California Architecture and Architects, No. 14.

ISBN: 0-940512-12-2

Hennessey + Ingalls
1254 3rd Street Promenade
Santa Monica CA 90401

Library of Congress Cataloging-in-Publication Data
Residential architecture in Southern California.

    Residential architecture in Southern California, 1939.
   Mediterranean to modern / [edited by Paul Robinson Hunter and Walter L. Reichardt].
        p.   cm.—(California architecture and architects; no. 14)

    Originally published: Residential architecture in Southern California. Los Angeles: Southern
California Chapter, American Institute of Architects, 1939.

    ISBN 0-940512-12-2 (trade paperbound)

    1. Architecture, Domestic—California, Southern.   2. Architecture, Modern—20th
century–California–California, Southern.   I. Hunter, Paul Robinson.   II. Reichardt, Walter L.
III. Title.   IV. Series.
NA7235.C22S6875 1998
728'. 09794'09041–dc21   98-6830

FOREWORD

The Southern California Chapter of the American Institute of Architects presents this book on Residential Architecture in response to an insistent public and professional demand.

The representative houses included herein cannot be considered as a complete pictorial review of the work of architects in this region. It is rather an indication of the trend in residential design and a record of the changes that have occurred during the past twenty years in owners' requirements and the architects' solutions.

A substantial number of the houses published have received recognition in nation-wide contests and in Honor Award Programs sponsored locally by the Southern California Chapter. Many equally meritorious houses are not included, and to the owners and architects we admit that it would indeed be a very simple matter to compile many more volumes of excellent examples of contemporary houses. The public and professional acceptance of this first effort will indicate the demand and need for further presentation of such material in book form.

Many members of the Chapter have assisted in the preparation of this book. To Paul Hunter and Walter Reichardt is due particular credit for their continuous effort over a period of time, and their consistent good judgment is evidenced in the final result.

The publication of these fine houses serves as a mark of recognition to those owners who by their intelligent and sympathetic cooperation have released for the benefit of all the best efforts of the architectural profession.

The material is arranged chronologically with brief introductory historical notes and occasional plans. The bulk of the material, however, consists of contemporary houses. The changes so evident in twenty years makes Ovid's two thousand year old statement most appropriate:

"My home, the city, and the image of well known places pass before my eyes; and each different event follows in its time."

President, Southern California Chapter,
The American Institute of Architects.

TABLE OF CONTENTS

THE MEDITERRANEAN INFLUENCE

THE CALIFORNIA HERITAGE

THE COLONIAL PRECEDENTS

THE CONTEMPORARY DEVELOPMENTS

THE MEDITERRANEAN INFLUENCE

California of the Spanish and Mexican periods was a sparsely settled country of small pueblos and large ranchos. The land was first developed through the zeal and efforts of the Franciscan Fathers who established twenty-one Missions extending from San Diego to San Francisco. While the Missions were the most important architectural structures of the time, many simple charming houses also were built during these periods. With heavy walls of sun dried bricks and roofs of hand made clay tiles, these houses were usually planned about an open square, or patio, with a continuous veranda upon which opened all of the rooms.

Contact with the American trading ships brought about a gradual introduction of Colonial woodwork which produced the more refined type of house so well exemplified in the work around Monterey. The beauty of these early houses, however, went unnoticed by the Americans who came in great numbers following the discovery of gold, and who carried with them the prevailing Victorian taste for elaborate, jig-saw decorated, wooden structures.

Shortly before the turn of the century, two types of houses quite different in character became popular. For the more pretentious residence, stucco was employed with design features adapted from the Franciscan Missions, a style well illustrated in the older portions of the Mission Inn at Riverside. For the smaller structures, the familiar one-story bungalow house of simple roof lines, wide eaves, and generous porches was developed.

A few years later a number of architects of eastern training and experience opened offices in Los Angeles. Through their influence the eastern interest in the traditional American Colonial, French, and English styles was reflected in California. It is likely that the residential work of this region would have continued similar to that of other parts of the United States had it not been for the introduction and wide acceptance of the Mediterranean styles— the Mexican, Spanish, and Italian.

The Panama Pacific Exposition of 1915 in San Diego brought to California for the first time a large grouping of buildings in the Spanish Colonial style. The architect for the Exposition, Bertram Goodhue, was one of the first to recognize the peculiar appropriateness of this style to the California setting. In 1900, he had traveled through Mexico preparing measured drawings for the book SPANISH COLONIAL ARCHITECTURE IN MEXICO by Sylvester Baxter, and later he designed the Pro Cathedral in Havana, Cuba, in the manner of the Mexican churches. The commission as architect for the Exposition gave Goodhue an opportunity to transplant to California this Spanish Colonial style. The effect was immediate and far reaching. It was difficult, however, for those unaccustomed to the style to adapt the character of the monumental exposition buildings to the more intimate needs of residences, and the first houses were full of compromises with the prevailing tastes, as well as being crude and clumsy due to the lack of trained craftsmen.

About 1920, a new and more graceful expression was given to the style by George Washington Smith in his work in Santa Barbara. He was influenced by the minor buildings and farm houses of Andalusia. Restrained and unpretentious houses of this kind, characterized by simple roof lines, richness of surface textures and materials, and an intimate relation to the garden by means of the patio, established the best type of Spanish architecture. For houses of a more formal and dignified appearance than could be afforded by these minor buildings of Spain, inspiration was found in the villas of northern Italy.

The Mediterranean style offered many opportunities in domestic architecture. It could be used with equal appropriateness for a small home or for a large residence in the grand manner. It was particularly suitable for hillside sites and permitted the arrangement of garden terraces on many levels. The widespread use of beautiful ceramic tiles and fine wrought ironwork developed craftsmen of great ability. The interiors were often exceedingly rich, and large mantels, massive furniture, and heavy draperies were frequently utilized. The gardens also drew upon Europe for inspiration for their extensive formal plans, for pools and fountains, and for long avenues of palm and cypress trees.

7

STREET SCENE   GRANADA

CITY HOUSE   RONDA

GARDEN   RONDA

To be seen in the street above are some of the characteristic features of the Spanish architecture which inspired the early Mediterranean work in California: the tile roofs, the plain wall surfaces, the elaborate doorways, and the extensive use of wrought iron for grilles and railings. Particularly appropriate are the enclosed gardens of Southern Spain, with their pools and fountains, steps and terraces, evergreen shrubs and vine covered pergolas, their decorative tiles and terra cotta pottery.

VILLA MONTEGUFANI   NEAR FLORENCE

VILLA COLAZZI   NEAR FLORENCE

While in the domestic architecture of Italy there is greater dignity and restraint than in the romantic and picturesque houses of Spain, there are also many gay and imaginative details to be found. In the palaces illustrated are to be seen the large doorways, the pedimented windows, the rusticated stone-work, and the open loggias so typical of Italian work. The magnificent gardens of Italy are justly famous, and on a scale seldom equalled in Spain. They are to be noted for their cascades and pools, monumental stairs, formal clipped hedges, long and impressive vistas, and great use of sculpture.

VILLA MEDICI   FLORENCE

WRIGHT LUDINGTON HOUSE   SANTA BARBARA   BERTRAM G. GOODHUE   ARCHITECT

Bertram Goodhue designed this residence, an early example of the Mediterranean type in California. Beyond the entrance door is the enclosed patio characteristic of Spanish houses; from this direct access may be had to the principal rooms on the first floor. The garden side opens upon a wide terrace, and has large arched windows and an overhanging second story supported by heavy wood beams.

J. P. JEFFERSON HOUSE   SANTA BARBARA

REGINALD D. JOHNSON   ARCHITECT

The award of the Gold Medal of The American Institute of Architects to this house in 1922 was indicative of the achievements in residential design at this time in Southern California. The plain wall surfaces of the facade are relieved by the concentrated ornament at the entrance, by the striped awnings and the wrought iron work at the windows and balconies, and by the carefully arranged planting. Landscape architecture by Paul Thiene.

CRAIG HEBERTON HOUSE   SANTA BARBARA   GEORGE WASHINGTON SMITH   ARCHITECT

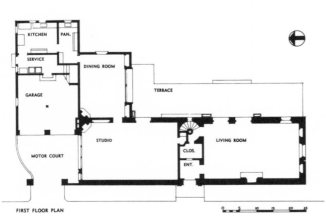

This house was originally designed by the architect as a home and studio for himself. The plain wall surfaces of the street front are in contrast with the detail about the entrance and the striking forms of the desert plants. The garden side is informal and opens upon a terrace. Its intimate and friendly character, clipped hedges, and tiled seats are reminiscent of Granada and Seville. The interiors have tiled floors, plain plastered walls, and dark stained ceiling beams. The furnishings were brought from Spain by the owner.

STREET ELEVATION

LIVING ROOM

I. EISNER HOUSE   LOS ANGELES   GORDON B. KAUFMANN   ARCHITECT

The Italian influence is evident in the stone trim about the entrance and in the quoins at the corners. The arched doorway and open loggia of the projecting wing, and the reflecting pool bordered by broad walks and planting area are well composed. Landscape architecture by Paul Thiene.

14

E. L. DOHENY RANCH   SANTA PAULA CANYON   WALLACE NEFF   ARCHITECT

A simplicity of architectural forms is evident in this rambling one-story ranch house built about three sides of a patio, and set in a thickly wooded grove. The long lines of the unusually low pitched tile roofs, supported on heavily buttressed walls, are broken by chimneys with hoods in an interesting variety of designs.

PIERPONT DAVIS HOUSE   LOS ANGELES

PIERPONT & WALTER S. DAVIS   ARCHITECT

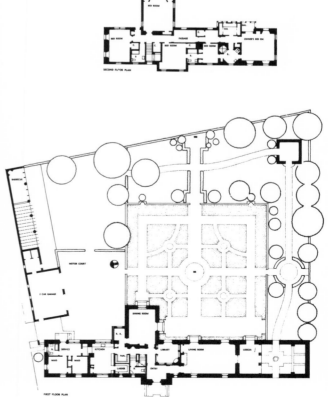

LIVING ROOM   PIERPONT DAVIS HOUSE

The formality of the Florentine villas is reflected in this Italian residence. Notable are its well spaced windows, heavily rusticated doorway, and simple roof line. The interiors with their rich furnishings and elaborate ceiling treatments have a beauty and authenticity rarely found. The principal rooms open upon the large enclosed garden.

WALLACE NEFF HOUSE   PASADENA

WALLACE NEFF   ARCHITECT

The dominant feature of the symmetrically composed front elevation is the deep shadowed second floor loggia, painted a turquoise blue. The dining room and entrance hall open upon a garden porch, whose white walls are accented by the colors of the brick floor; wood ceilings, and potted plants. Landscape architecture by A. E. Hanson.

A covered passage, through which the stone paved drive leads from the street to the motor court, connects the house and garage of this Spanish type residence. Prominent on the front elevation is an overhanging balcony of roughly adzed posts and beams. The foreyard planting is an early example of ivy used as a ground cover. Furniture of several periods is harmoniously combined in the interiors. Landscape architecture by Yoch and Council.

R. B. FUDGER HOUSE   LOS ANGELES   ROLAND E. COATE   ARCHITECT

HOMER SAMUELS HOUSE   LOS ANGELES

The white walls of the entrance garden form a pleasant background for the trailing vines and espaliered plants in the narrow borders. The cool covered passage with its vista of a sunlit garden thru the delicate tracery of the gates recaptures the charm of the Italian villas. Landscape architecture by Yoch and Council. The dark work and furnishing of the living room are in striking contrast to the white of the walls and the large mantel.

C. V. CRAWFORD HOUSE   LOS ANGELES

GORDON B. KAUFMANN   ARCHITECT

An extensive use of potted plants and fine olive trees break the strong horizontal lines of this house, which architecturally is in the best Spanish tradition. The upper terrace provides a fine view of the lower garden, with its gay fountain and small planting areas surrounded by gravel walks. Landscape architecture by Yoch and Council.

WILLIAM S. McCAY SR. HOUSE   PASADENA

WILLIAM S. McCAY   ARCHITECT

The lean-to roof, the heavy wood beams, and the painted dado of this house express something of the crudity of the Mexican farmhouses. In the same spirit is the interior, with simple plaster walls, brick floor, and natural wood ceiling.

DONALD DICKEY GUEST HOUSE   OJAI

PALMER SABIN   ARCHITECT

An old grape arbor and fine live oak trees form the background for this guest house on a large ranch. In the use of adobe and heavy wood framing, a successful effort has been made to recall the character of the work of the early builders.

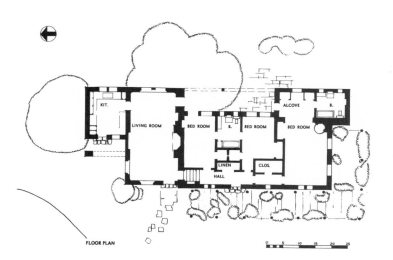

FLOOR PLAN

WILLIAM H. BLISS HOUSE   SANTA BARBARA   CARLETON M. WINSLOW   ARCHITECT

Typical of the setting of many California houses is the location of this residence among live oak trees, with a view of mountains in the background. It stands as one of the best examples of work influenced by the San Diego Exposition of 1915. The garden elevation which faces south has a monumental character in the broad sweeping steps, the repetition of arched openings, and the use of fine wrought iron in the window grilles and balcony railings.

R. B. HONEYMAN HOUSE   REGINALD D. JOHNSON   ARCHITECT

Above: A detail of many Mediterranean houses and a striking feature of this one is the exterior stairway with its stepped parapet and potted plants accenting the simplicity of the wall above. Landscaping by Katherine Bashford.

DOROTHY ARZNER GARDEN   YOCH & COUNCIL

Below: This garden is a fine example of the successful combination of landscaping and architecture. Built on several levels, the parapet walls of the garden form a background for the interesting masses of the planting.

ENTRANCE DOORWAY   McKINLEY HOUSE   MONTEREY

Crisp details and simple forms of Colonial inspiration have made this house one of the architectural showplaces of old Monterey. The beautifully proportioned entry door and moulded trim are seen to advantage against the plain plaster wall. This balcony is an example of the use of a facia board covering the cantilevered beam ends.

THE CALIFORNIA HERITAGE

The Mediterranean style was at the height of its popularity during the early Twenties and was regarded by the public and architects alike as the most appropriate expression for architecture in California. It was in keeping with a widespread effort to identify California with Mexico and Spain, and to give to it historical associations comparable to those of the Colonial States. The use of Spanish place names, the encouragement of Latin customs and fiestas, and the interest in early history were indicative of a desire to create an old world atmosphere.

For many people, however, these romantically designed Mediterranean houses necessitated too great a break with the background and traditions familiar to most Americans. The style, too, began to enter upon a period of excesses. Plaster of extravagant texture and garish color was not uncommon. Window and door openings were of all sizes and shapes. Facades were sometimes of affected severity, sometimes of confused exuberance, with grilles, tilework, and round towers in profusion.

About 1925 certain architects became interested in the little known early residential architecture that was native to California, and began to draw inspiration from the old buildings of that period. The best historical examples are in Monterey, dating from about 1815 to 1855; and while the name Monterey was given to the style, houses of similar character are to found all along the coast.

The Monterey house was essentially a thick walled adobe brick structure with considerable woodwork of Colonial design, which was either brought about the Horn by ship or was made locally by carpenters trained in the New England traditions. The most distinguishing feature was the projection on the main facade of a covered wood balcony, although one and two story porches on several sides of the house were also common. The adobe bricks were covered with mud plaster and whitewashed. The windows and doors were Colonial in character, the windows being set flush on the outside to afford a reveal on the interior. Shutters were used on both the exterior and interior. The roofs were gabled and hipped and covered either with tile or with hand split shakes, depending upon whether the locality could better furnish clay or wood. Originally there were only a few stairways—most of the second floor rooms being reached by outside stairs and balconies. In the interiors, the rooms were simple with white plastered walls, occasionally papered, tile and wood floors, and small wood mantels.

A connecting link existed between the earlier work and a desire for more restrained, simple homes, and an appreciation for the simplicity of mass and detail and the utter absence of ornamentation of the older California houses had a beneficial effect. In the new work the balcony was made the feature of the style. Houses were usually white, and color was added in shutters and details. Front doors were recessed and the windows made double hung. White painted brick was introduced and the use of boarding became widespread.

Most of the houses, like their predecessors were placed on level sites. Olive and live oak trees, broad leaved plants, and ground covers were used about the houses. Picket fences were added to the familiar accessories of potted shrubs and vines.

While the design features of the Monterey houses were quite uniform in character, the style permitted the blending of details from other periods. Victorian touches in the form of caps, brackets, and band sawn edgings have been added as decoration. In place of wood posts and railings on the balconies the use of painted cast iron similar to that found in New Orleans has given a certain sophistication to the recent work.

ORTEGA HOUSE   SANTA BARBAR

This adobe house with a projecting balcony across the second story, double hung windows, wood trim, and a shingle roof of steeper pitch than that of the earlier Spanish houses, has been a popular source of inspiration. The exterior plaster is whitewashed and the sash and doors painted. On pages 31 and 43 are modern adaptations.

LUGO HOUSE   BELL

This house is one of the few remaining examples about Los Angeles of an adobe with wide two story proches. The simple wood posts, the balustrade, and the pleasant, double pitched roof are outstanding features. On pages 32, 35, and 42 are modern adaptations.

CENTINELA RANCHO   INGLEWOOD

The generous porch along the front of this house mark it as one of the most successful of the one story type. The slight pediment treatment over the openings is characteristic of the period. The central portion is of adobe and originally had a flat rush covered roof in place of the present pitched one. The wing at the right is of later date. On pages 30, 40, and 41 are modern adaptations.

BING CROSBY RANCH HOUSE   RANCHO SANTA FE   LILLIAN J. RICE   ARCHITECT

The original adobe of this old rancho, which
bears a close resemblance to the Centinela
Rancho shown on the preceding page, has
been restored and added to by the present
owner. The simple architectural lines are
relieved only by the planting and by the
detail about the porch openings. The living room with its open ceiling construc-
tion has been decorated by Harold Grieve.

F. L. OLMSTEAD HOUSE   PALOS VERDES

MYRON HUNT & H. C. CHAMBERS   ARCHITECTS

Typical of the early California houses is this long one story tile roofed house set among tall eucalyptus trees. A somewhat rugged character is given by the heavy champfered posts and beams and the coarse stonework of the walls and paving. Landscape Architecture by the Olmstead Brothers.

H. J. SCHOTT HOUSE   LOS ANGELES   WILLIAM H. HARRISON   ARCHITECT

This pleasant example of a Monterey type house is completely enclosed by a picket fence. Accentuating the long lines of the main block of the house are one story wings at either end. The balcony railing has a diagonal cross design as a variation from the more usual vertical balusters. The herringbone panels of the entrance door are to be found in many New England houses. Landscape architecture by Katherine Bashford.

H. B. PERRIN HOUSE PASADENA

GARVIN HODSON ARCHITECT

The street side presents a typical example of the Monterey house with white plastered adobe walls, a second story projecting balcony, large and symmetrically placed windows, doors with deep reveals, a dark shake roof, and a simple chimney. The shutters and trim about the windows, the porch posts and railing, the lantern post, and even the picket fence above the low cobblestone wall show the influence of the Colonial woodwork of New England.

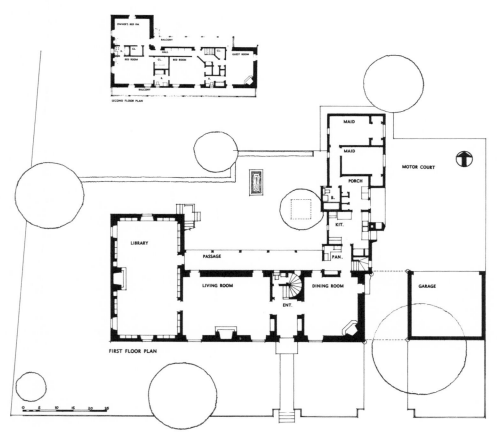

Above is the patio side of the house with a two story porch supported on slender posts and an outside stair to the second floor. The flagstone paving and small stone well are softened by informal planting of trees and bushes.

Below is the library, a white plastered room with a light colored wood ceiling. Between the deep reveals of the windows are bookcases which extend from floor to ceiling. Most of the furniture is of the late Colonial period.

W. C. McDUFFIE HOUSE PASADENA

REGINALD D. JOHNSON ARCHITECT

The combination of the arched loggia and the second story covered balcony with the informal planting gives the garden side of this house an interest and charm that recalls the days of the early ranchos. The entrance elevation on the motor court is dominated by the projecting balcony with decorative wrought iron panels in the railing. Landscape architecture by Katherine Bashford.

JAMES IRVINE HOUSE   PASADENA   H. ROY KELLEY   ARCHITECT

The use of two story brick piers as a strong vertical accent is a variation of the usual balcony treatment. A pleasant feature is the continuation of the porch about two sides of the house. The sunlit terraces and garden pool are shaded by a carob tree. Landscape Architecture by Yoch and Council.

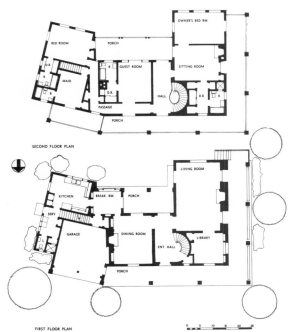

F. M. TAYLOR & H. C. LIPPIATT HOUSE   LOS ANGELES

ROLAND E. COATE   ARCHITECT

This white walled, tile roofed house is an example of the harmonious blending of several styles of architecture. The decorative iron work of the balcony, painted a light green, is reminiscent of New Orleans, while the wrought iron window grilles are of Spanish character. The entrance door with its side lights and transom is of New England inspiration.

JAMES P. MACKEL HOUSE   SAN MARINO   DOUGLAS H. MCLELLAN   ARCHITECT

The wide porch is a pleasing variation from the usual balcony treatment of two story houses and gives a hospitable appearance. A feature of the plan is the first floor bedroom in a wing separate from the rest of the house. In the garden is a board and batten guest house with barbecue fireplace on the porch.

SECOND FLOOR PLAN

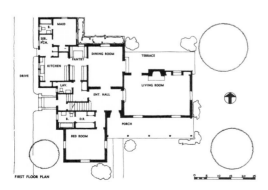

FIRST FLOOR PLAN

BEN R. MEYER RANCH HOUSE   SANTA BARBARA   GORDON B. KAUFMANN   ARCHITECT

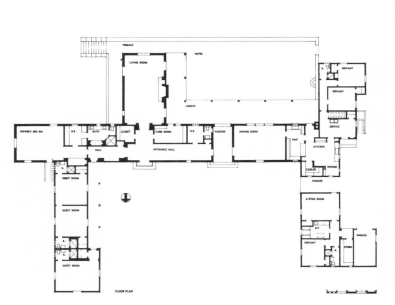

This rambling ranch house of open plan conforms to the landscape and to the informal living requirements. Each room has access to the large central court or to the patio with its fine ocean view. The early California inspiration may be seen in the general character of the long low roof lines, and in such details as the rough hewn posts and beams of the covered porch, and the wood window grilles. Landscape architecture by Paul Thiene.

KUBIC GLASMAN HOUSE   LOS ANGELES   H. C. NEWTON & ROBERT D. MURRAY   ARCHITECTS

This small ranch house is placed on the side of a hill against a background of tall eucalyptus trees. The broad sturdy chimney is in keeping with the low lines of the house. The walls are of vertical boarding and on the porch the roof rafters are left exposed.

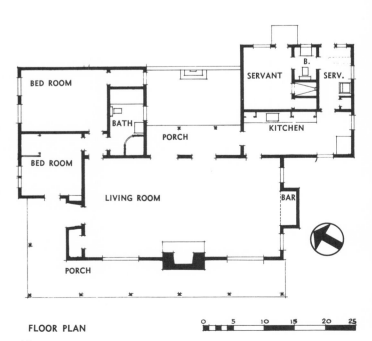

FLOOR PLAN

0   5   10   15   20   25

40

PRENTISS FULMOR HOUSE   PASADENA

GARRETT VAN PELT & GEORGE LIND   ARCHITECTS

The spirit of the early California work is caught in this house
at the base of the mountains. The band-sawn caps of the porch
posts are Victorian in character, and the windows have the
slight pediments at the head so often found in earlier examples.

G. CHAPLIN HOUSE   BEVERLY HILLS   ROY SELDON PRICE   ARCHITECT

Above: The entrance doorway of this simple house is covered by a luxuriant wisteria vine supported on a cantilevered trellis. Planting successfully screens the service wing. Landscape architecture by B. M. Purdy.

Below: A different treatment of a two story porch is illustrated here. Brick piers and balustrades are used on the first floor, while on the second floor are wood posts and railing.

T. N. ST. HILL HOUSE   PASADENA   DONALD McMURRAY

FRANCIS STEVENS HOUSE   PASADENA   MARSTON & MAYBURY   ARCHITECTS

POTTER BOWLES HOUSE   EMERALD BAY   DONALD B. KIRBY   ARCHITECT

Above: A use of strong horizontal lines characterizes this Monterey type house. Pairs of large French doors open upon the terrace across the front. In the foreground a pergola of logs screens the cobblestone retaining wall.

Below: Featured by the treatment of a two story porch with double posts, this residence is placed against a hill covered with eucalyptus trees and commands a sweeping view of the ocean.

43

CYRIL CHAPPELLET HOUSE   LOS ANGELES   H. ROY KELLEY   ARCHITECT

The repetition of horizontal lines in this house creates an air of quiet and repose. The utter simplicity of the wood posts and balcony railing is pleasantly relieved by potted plants secured in metal holders. The projecting wings and a large olive tree shelter the patio from the wind. Landscape architecture by Bashford and Barlow.

J. BARBER HOUSE   PASADENA   ROLAND E. COATE ARCHITECT

J. W. BIXBY HOUSE   PASADENA   ROLAND E. COATE   ARCHITECT

The early California interiors reflect
much of the Mediterranean influence,
with their use of heavy, dark-stained
beams, plain plaster walls, openings
without casings, and simple mantels.

45

DOORWAY OF PETERSON MUSTARD MANSION
SMYRNA DELAWARE

THE AMERICAN COLONIAL PRECEDENTS

The widespread interest in the Monterey style, with its emphasis on the use of New England Colonial detail in the wood work, gave a new impetus to the study of Colonial architecture itself. The idea of perpetuating California as a Spanish province had begun to lose its earlier romantic appeal, and there was a growing desire to be in the current of the general architectural trends of the United States. Articles in magazines and the publication of new books of fine photographs and measured drawings on Colonial architecture was awakening a greater appreciation of the beauty and charm of this work.

The best use of Colonial in California has been as an adaptation rather than a literal copying of earlier work. Attempted copies have produced houses which have not seemed particularly at home. In this adaptation the gracious, dignified houses of the Middle Atlantic States have been turned to most frequently for inspiration, rather than the somewhat austere places of New England or the porticoed, Greek revival mansions of the South. The refinement and delicacy of the small houses of the late Georgian period in England also have been drawn upon.

In tempering Colonial work to California traditions, certain changes may be noted. In place of the snow shedding pitches of the east, the wood shingled roofs have adhered to the low pitches of earlier California work, in both hipped and gabled types. Instead of being left natural stone or brick, the wall surfaces have generally been painted, usually white, occasionally shades of tan, green, or grey. Dormer windows, practically unknown in Monterey work, have been introduced to break the eave and cornice lines, particularly in minor wings. Colonial details have been drawn upon in meeting the increasingly popular taste for bay windows. About entrances and porches there has been a general use of lattice work both in wood and iron.

The plans, however, have not undergone a great deal of change. They have continued to be quite open in character, usually L or U shaped, either about a patio or an enclosed garden, with the principal rooms facing south.

Interiors in the Colonial manner have been particularly prized as a fitting background for most types of furniture. There has been a great use of wood in wainscots, casework, and in the paneling of entire walls. Stair halls have received much attention, and many beautiful railings of wood and metal balusters have been produced.

The close relationship between the house and garden has continued. The character, however, has been intimate rather than extensive as in the formal gardens of the Mediterranean period. Espaliered trees and vines and broad paved terraces with boxed shrubs have been frequently used as decorative features. In the accessories of the garden, the tables, chairs, and benches, there has been a pleasing delicacy of detail.

CITY HOUSE   GERMANTOWN PA.

DOORWAY   CHARLESTON N. C.

As shown in these illustrations, the architecture of the American Colonies developed a great variety of expressions. It embraced such diverse types of residential work as the informal rambling country place, the small town house, and the stately city mansion, and employed stone, brick, plaster, and wood as building materials.

HOUSE ON THE WISSAHICKON   NEAR PHILADELPHIA

DETAIL "AMSTEL HOUSE"   NEW CASTLE DE

H. S. PARSONS HOUSE   PASADENA

PALMER SABIN   ARCHITECT

This house expresses Colonial traditions in the symmetry of the street elevation and in its details. The California influence is shown by the enclosed patio, by the low pitched roof, and by the bright colors of the white walls and yellow shutters.

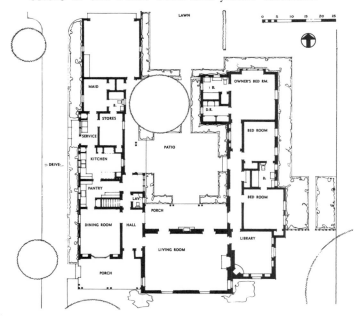

49

GARDEN ELEVATION

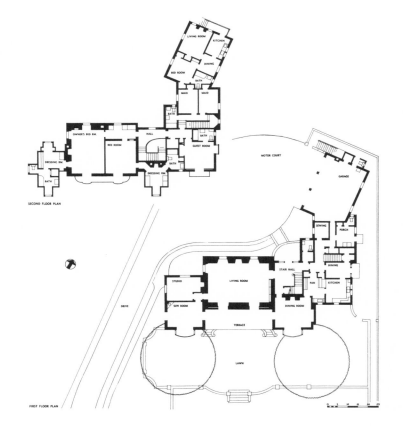

One of the finest examples of the Georgian and French influences, this house is noteworthy for its beautiful proportions, formal placement of windows, and its austere roof and chimneys. Although characterized by simplicity of form, great attention has been paid to detail, as in the entrance porch and open sun room at the end of the terrace. Landscape architecture by Yoch and Council.

R. B. FUDGER HOUSE
BEVERLY HILLS

ROLAND E. COATE
ARCHITECT

NELSON PERRIN HOUSE   PASADENA   WILLIAM S. McCAY   ARCHITECT

A brick walk leads up to this small house of Regency inspiration with its well designed cornice and delicate post-Adam iron railing. The finely proportioned entrance has a delicate fan in the arch above the door. The living room is distinguished by its high ceiling, large windows, and the careful detail of the marble mantel. Landscape architecture by Yoch and Council.

M. & G. HOUSTON HOUSE   LOS ANGELES

H. ROY KELLEY   ARCHITECT

Colonial in inspiration this white brick house is considerably lower and broader in proportion than similar houses along the Eastern seaboard. The large bay windows of the living and dining rooms are features.

Although placed at the front of the house, the garage is inconspicuous and well screened by a pergola and planting. Landscape architecture by Bashford and Barlow.

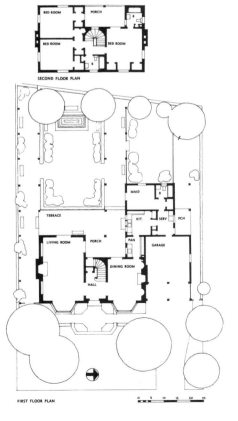

DAVID O. SELZNICK HOUSE   BEVERLY HILLS   ROLAND E. COATE   ARCHITECT

The Colonial work of the Middle Atlantic States
is recalled in this house which has been adapted
to California through the low pitch of the roof
and the white painted brick walls. The semi-
circular entrance porch is noteworthy because
of the fine lines and the beauty of its ironwork.

SIDNEY R. FRANCIS HOUSE   PASADENA   REGINALD D. JOHNSON   ARCHITECT

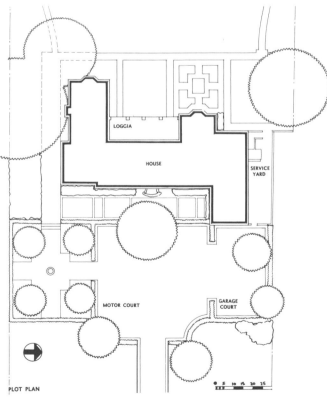

PLOT PLAN

A formal treatment of horizontal and vertical lines distinguishes this brick house with its fine use of pilasters. The dark entrance door contrasts with the light tone of the stone detail. Landscape architecture by Bashford and Barlow.

55

A HOUSE IN BEVERLY HILLS

DOUGLAS HONNOLD & GEORGE V. RUSSELL   ARCHITECTS

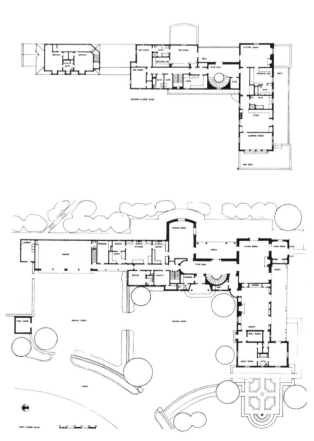

In this house is to be found the delicacy and refinement of the late Georgian period of England. Much of the charm of the interiors is due to the height of the ceilings and to the simplicity and restraint of the furnishings. Landscape architecture by Tommy Tomson; interiors by Harriet Shellenberger.

CHARLES S. PADDOCK HOUSE   PASADENA

MARSTON & MAYBURY   ARCHITECTS

A feeling of balance and repose pervades this house despite the unsymmetrical character of the main block.   The entrance has an interesting treatment of rusticated brick work.

58

VERNON LARSEN HOUSE   PASADENA

EDGAR BISSANTZ   ARCHITECT

Dignity is achieved in this small house by the symmetrical treatment of the center block balanced by lattice treated wings. The design of the cornice and the entry door are noteworthy. The louvered doors with concealed screens allow for summer ventilation. Landscape architecture by Katherine Bashford.

ARTHUR SMILEY HOUSE   LOS ANGELES

ROLAND E. COATE   ARCHITECT

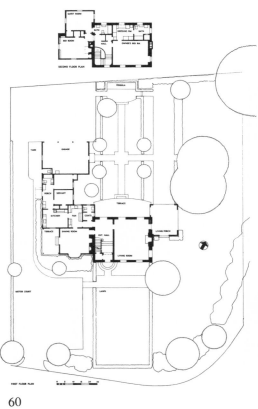

The formal center unit of this house is of a warm gray stone whose texture contrasts interestingly with the less formal wings of heavy white shakes. The orderly spacing of the windows of the center unit and the beautifully proportioned wrought iron porch contribute greatly to the success of the house. Landscape architecture by Bashford and Barlow.

ALEXANDER KIAM HOUSE   LOS ANGELES   DOUGLAS HONNOLD & GEORGE V. RUSSELL   ARCHITECTS

A quiet dignity is achieved in the simplicity of the gable roof and in the spacing and repetition of the large French doors which open upon the garden terrace. The study, with delicate wood paneling, is painted a light green, and has a light colored marble fireplace surround of bold design.

JOHN R. LITTLE HOUSE   LA CANADA

EDGAR BISSANTZ   ARCHITECT

Appropriate to the setting is this warm gray plaster house with extremely simple roof lines. The white recessed entrance door treatment and the large double hung windows are of Colonial character. In the interiors, the wood wainscot and ceiling are to be noted, as are the wood louvre shutters used in place of draperies. Landscape architecture by Bashford and Barlow.

63

SAMUEL BEHRENDT HOUSE   BEVERLY HILLS   SUMNER SPAULDING   ARCHITECT

The rough textured wall surface of this shake house provides a pleasant background for the vine covered trellis design of the recessed entrance porch. The principal rooms of both floors open upon the garden.

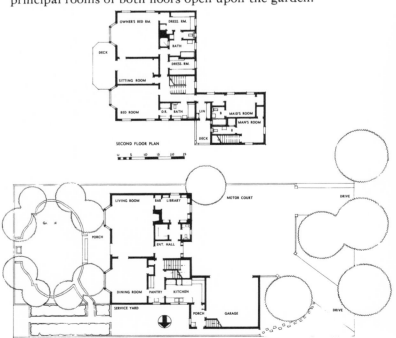

SIDNEY FRANKLIN HOUSE   MARSTON & MAYBURY   ARCHITECTS

Above: Shaded by the house and trees is this pleasant little flagstone paved terrace whose important feature is the lead fountain set against the arcaded brick wall. Landscape architecture by Katherine Bashford.

Below: At the end of a garden walk is this graceful piece of garden furniture, with richly carved back and curving ends.

GARDEN BENCH   **FRANK BADEN**

H. W. MAXWELL HOUSE   SAN MARINO

FREDERIC BARIENBROCK   ARCHITECT

A. H. BRANNON HOUSE   LA HABRA   W. H. HARRISON   ARCHITECT

Above: In pleasant combination for outdoor living are the covered porch and patio. The tiled flower sink is convenient for house and garden use.

Below: The stone walls and extensive use of wood detail in this house suggest its Colonial sources. The flagstone terrace across the front leads to the entrance.

C. R. JOHNSON HOUSE   WHITTIER   ARTHUR R. HUTCHASON   ARCHITECT

E. P. CLARK HOUSE   SUMNER SPAULDING

Above: Set effectively in a smooth plaster wall is this gracious entrance of Colonial inspiration with its paneled recess, small transom lights, and hinged shutters.

Below: Completely enclosed by the walls of the house, this inviting patio is used as an outdoor living and dining room. The great vine with its delicate and luxuriant foliage provides shade from the summer sun.

FRANCIS GRIFFIN HOUSE   BEVERLY HILLS

SUMNER SPAULDING   ARCHITECT

Planned for outdoor living is this broad terrace opening off the living room and dining room. A covered porch with informal trellised vine covered walls affords shade from the sun. Steps flanked by boxed trees lead down from the terrace to the lawn area, bordered by clipped hedges and trees. Landscape architecture by Hammond Sadler.

CONTEMPORARY DEVELOPMENTS

The term contemporary is used to designate those houses built during the past few years in which a sincere effort has been made to meet the changed requirements and point of view of today. While many influences have combined in bringing about these changes, certain ones are outstanding. A growing appreciation of the importance of comfort and workability has been met by a more intensive use of space and a greater flexibility in planning, and has brought about a departure from the concept of "pure" style and a release from the forms of traditional architecture. An increased interest in the out-of-doors has resulted in creating larger living and playing areas adjacent to the house, and bringing the out-of-doors indoors. Other influences, such as expositions, travel, and advertising have stimulated the acceptance of new ideas.

For the purpose of simplification the material presented under the heading of contemporary may be roughly divided into two groups: the first, which borrows from the past and is traditional in character; and the second, which makes a conscious effort to free itself from the use of historical forms. The variety and freedom from uniformity shown in these houses indicate that the present period is one of transition, similar to past periods during which new social, aesthetic, and structural problems were being solved.

The first group retains and adapts certain features of traditional work, incorporating at the same time the new ideas which have become generally recognized as essential to more comfortable living. In the process of adaptation to this region the traditional forms have undergone simplification, even elimination, and in many cases these forms appear only in details and accessories. The Mediterranean style, though seldom used today, is still an influence. The early California and Colonial styles, however, form the basis for most of the traditional work. Many houses have as their unsuspected but direct ancestor that simple and unassuming house which was developed contemporaneously with Mission architecture, namely, the California bungalow. Characteristic features of the first group are the low pitch of the hip roofs, the increased projection of the eaves, and the larger window and door openings for more convenient access to the gardens and patios.

Fundamental to an appreciation of the work of the second group is an understanding of what is meant by the term modern. Modern is not a style, it is a basic idea. As set forth by Louis Sullivan, "Form follows function and function creates form." Less succinctly expressed, this means that a house is created to perform a certain function, that the important elements of the plan should not be modified by the exigencies of a given style, and that the exterior should express the interior form. Unless identical in plan, location, and requirements, no two houses should look alike.

The true architecture of every period has been a reflection of that period: its customs and traditions, its climatic conditions and available building materials. This architecture, therefore, loses significance when artificially grafted upon another age with different ideals and requirements. Modern architects believe that the historical styles in reflecting the life of their periods were "modern," and in this respect they are continuing to work with the same objectives that have produced the important work of the past.

A departure from hard and fast rules of architectural styles is shown in the work of both contemporary groups, which also demonstrates that the present day requirements of the individual may be met in many ways. It may be equally appropriate for buildings to have various window treatments, either large or small, roofs that are either pitched or flat, exteriors of stucco, wood, brick or stone, while the interiors may be equally free in treatment. What is of great importance, however, is that there be an intelligent use of the different elements that enter into the design of the building, as well as a sympathetic and proper use of all building materials.

H. H. BRALY HOUSE   LOS ANGELES

GORDON B. KAUFMANN   ARCHITECT

The long lines of this low lying house
of concrete blocks are suggestive of the
Spanish and Mexican periods, although
the house itself is free from traditional
details. The arched opening of the
entrance has a pleasing grille in wood.

SUMNER SPAULDING HOUSE   BEVERLY HILLS   SUMNER SPAULDING   ARCHITECT

The completely enclosed patio is the living center of this house. Large sliding doors at the end of either loggia afford both cross ventilation and protection from the wind; to the north may be had a view out upon open country. Due to the slope of the property, the entrance and garages are located on the first floor, while the living quarters are on the second floor. The fresco adds an interesting note to the simple wall. Landscape architecture by Ralph Cornell.

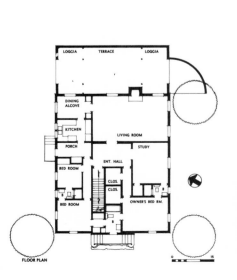

DANIEL BURNHAM HOUSE   PASADENA

PALMER SABIN   ARCHITECT

This house was so planned that a fine group of eucalyptus trees might be preserved in the center of the patio. The solarium, an unusual feature, is virtually a glass en- closed garden with continuous windows and skylights on the patio side. Inside planting strips are placed along the windows. Landscape architecture by Katherine Bashford.

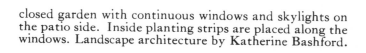

MAURICE SAETA HOUSE   LOS ANGELES   WINCHTON L. RISLEY   ARCHITECT

The success of this hillside house is due in part to the careful consideration given the relationship of the house to its site. Full advantage of the fine view has been taken by the location of the pleasant terrace and the generous size and spacing of the windows.

DAVID WALTER HOUSE   ARCADIA

MARSTON & MAYBURY   ARCHITECT

This rambling home with its pleasant motor court, inviting covered porch, and long simple roof lines is characteristic of many ranch houses. The service wing is separated from the main portion of the house by a covered passage, leading to the garden beyond.

FREDERIC BECK HOUSE   LOS ANGELES   H. ROY KELLEY   ARCHITECT

Fitting nicely into its background this
small house makes pleasant use of a
covered porch. A painted dado gives
interest to the porch, as does the use
of vertical boards in place of plaster.

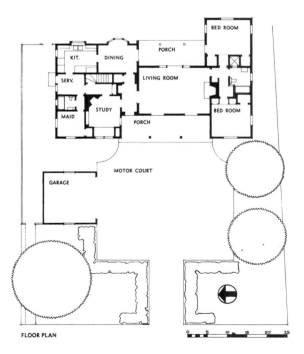

FLOOR PLAN

HOYNE WELLS HOUSE   SIERRA MADRE   GRAHAM LATTA   ARCHITEC

In this long simple house the character of the early board and
batten ranch houses has been used as a background for fine old
furniture. From the screen porch off the living room a magnificent view of the mountains may be had. In the interiors the
rafters are exposed, and in the bedroom the deep window reveal
permits the use of inside shutters.

FLOOR PLAN   0   5   10   15   20   25

JOHN GREGG HOUSE   ARCADIA   GARRETT VAN PELT & GEORGE LIND   ARCHITECTS

The entrance porch of this pleasant brick house
has slightly curved arches suggestive of New
England. An attractive feature is the continuous
covered porch about three sides of the courtyard.

HAROLD G. SPIELMAN HOUSE   PALM SPRINGS   HAROLD G. SPIELMAN   ARCHITECT

The L shaped porch is a most livable feature of this
week-end house in the desert. The use of a cement
slab foundation permits the house to be built close to
the ground. An interesting roof profile is created by
increasing the pitch slightly over the central portion.

FLOOR PLAN

SEELEY MUDD HOUSE   **CARPINTERIA**

RALPH C. FLEWELLING   ARCHITECT

From the living room of this board and
batten beach house access may be had
either to the porch overlooking the ocean
or to the brick paved courtyard, sheltered by walls from the ocean breezes.
Landscape architecture by B. M. Purdy.

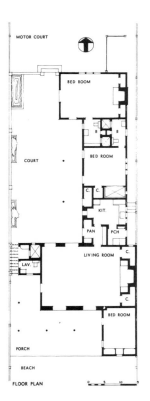

A. B. WELLS HOUSE   RANCHO SANTA FE

PALMER SABIN   ARCHITEC

Situated on a level site at the edge of a mesa, this U shaped house overlooks Rancho Santa Fe. A magnificent view of the distant mountains may be had from the covered passage in the center of the house, and large doors can be closed across it to protect the court from the ocean winds. The interiors are rich in the use of wood, and their spaciousness and rather formal furnishings create an atmosphere of pleasant country living.

J. P. CLAPP HOUSE   PASADENA

WINCHTON L. RISLEY   ARCHITECT

The outstanding feature of this interestingly planned
house is the patio which is illustrated in the frontispiece.
A close relationship between house and garden is obtained
by opening the dining room and guest suite upon the patio
and by making the other rooms accessible to terraces.
The house is preceded by a large walled-in motor court
with the garage so arranged as to screen the motor yard.

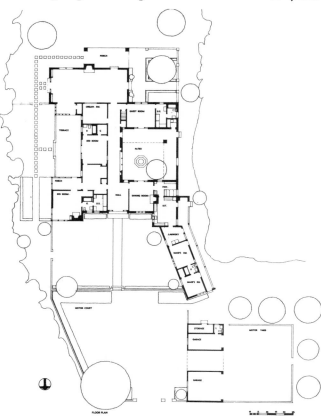

W. F. CARVER HOUSE   LOS ANGELES   ALLEN McGILL   ARCHITECT

This vine covered white brick house has
been placed close to the street to take advantage of level ground on a hillside. The
pergola of the flagstone entrance porch forms
an interesting pattern of light and shade,
and provides a pleasant informal note.

R. CAMPBELL HOUSE   SAN MARINO   WITMER & WATSON   ARCHITECTS

By placing the garage at the front
of this house, the rear of the property is left entirely free for garden
treatment.   The recessed wood
paneled entrance door with its side
lights, is effectively framed by two
large orange trees.

Protected from the street by trees and planting, this house has a pleasant air of seclusion. The inviting vista of a brick walk and a covered porch lead one from the motor court to the entrance doorway. The enclosed porch adjoining the living room is a livable and comfortable feature.

H. FULLERTON HOUSE   PASADENA   JONATHAN RING   ARCHITECT

SARAH E. McGOWAN HOUSE   RANCHO SANTA FE

WINCHTON L. RISLEY   ARCHITECT

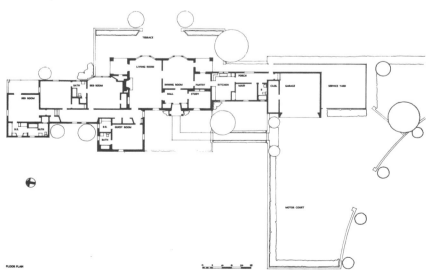

FLOOR PLAN

This low rambling country house owes much of its charm and dignity to its good proportions, generous scale, and simple roof lines. The inviting approach to the sheltered doorway, and the effective massing of the planting are to be noted.

MELVIN GARLOUGH HOUSE   SAN MARINO

MELVIN GARLOUGH   ARCHIT T

Interesting contrasts are to be found between the dark roof, shutters, and ivy foreyard, and the white walls of this crisply detailed wood house. The compact plan is well arranged for easy access to all rooms. The attractive patio for outdoor living and dining and the covered connection with the garage are both pleasant and convenient.

BEN H. O'CONNOR HOUSE   SAN MARINO   BEN H. O'CONNOR   ARCHITECT

A low wall and clipped hedge separate the motor court from the entry garden, shown in the lower picture. The symmetrical placing of the windows in the main block gives a slightly formal air which is modified by the low lying garage wing. Landscape architecture by Tommy Tomson.

HAL SMITH HOUSE   BALBOA   DONALD B. KIRBY   ARCHITECT

Clean cut lines and an informal atmosphere
characterize this comfortable looking beach
house. A large window in the living room looks
out on the sunny brick terrace, and the bed
rooms of the upper story open upon a sun deck.

I. L. BRYNER HOUSE   PASADENA   ROLAND E. COATE   ARCHITECT

Above: Of unusual width and length this low pergola suggests comfortable outdoor living. Vines form beautiful light patterns on the walls and pavement. At the far end the beams are spaced to accommodate the branches of the tree.

Below: The curved entrance steps and brick walls are embellished by the evergreen shrubs and potted plants which serve as a pleasant introduction to the visitor as well as to partially screen the house from the street.

S. B. GRAVES HOUSE   WINCHTON L. RISLEY   ARCHITECT

89

W. T. WALKER HOUSE   PALM SPRINGS   CHARLES O. MATCHAM   ARCHITECT

The living room of the guest house has sliding doors and screens which open the entire side of the room upon a small terrace with a tennis court in the foreground. The broad opening is protected from the sun by a colored awning which extends out to shade the terrace.

E. C. ANTHONY HOUSE   PALM SPRINGS   CHARLES O. MATCHAM   ARCHITECT

The long low lines of the house ar typical of the desert homes nea Palm Springs. The concrete block are painted an off-white, and a dad of sage green is carried around th house and the garage wing, whic are connected by a covered passag(

JEANNETTE DRAKE HOUSE   PASADENA

EDGAR BISSANTZ   ARCHITECT

The oriental character of this house is achieved by the extreme simplicity of the roof, the flare of the ridge line, the generous eave projections, the round windows, and the unusual planting. In the interior the char- acter is maintained by the occasional use of oriental accessories. The compact rectangular plan affords easy access from the entry hall to each room of the house. Landscape architecture by Roma Coolidge Mulvihill.

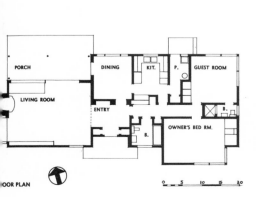

ROBERT E. BROOKER HOUSE   ARCADIA

THEODORE CRILEY, JR.   ARCHITECT

Much of the interest of this house is in the use of color and materials. The chimney is of natural brick, the plaster trim and door of light and dark shades of terra cotta, and the soffit of the eaves a blue-green. The den is treated with natural finished redwood boards.

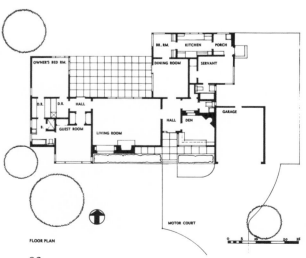

FLOOR PLAN

LOUISA CARPENTER HOUSE   PALM SPRINGS   DOUGLAS HONNOLD & GEORGE V. RUSSELL   ARCHITECTS

The sliding doors of the living room opening make possible a very close relationship between the indoor and outdoor living areas of this house. The long
horizontal lines of the dark tile roof and the light sand colored walls fit in well
with the desert background. Situated on a large piece of property, this house
has ample space for a motor court, sun yard, broad terrace, and swimming pool

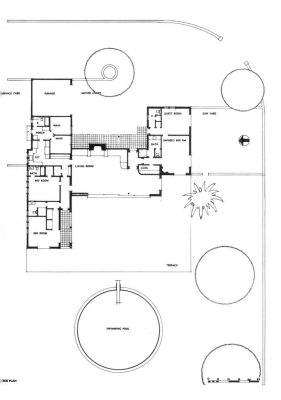

HAROLD S. ANDERSON HOUSE   LOS ANGELES

SUMNER SPAULDING   ARCHITECT

The extreme simplicity of the motor court elevation with its projecting entry hood, glass brick panel, and clipped hedges give this house a formal and dignified aspect. The garden side is less formal with large openings, and covered porches affording a full view of the valley below. Much of the furniture is built-in and the hand-woven fabrics are of interesting texture and color. Interiors by Donald Deskey. Landscape architecture by Hammond Sadler.

MOYE W. STEPHENS HOUSE   LA VERNE

THEODORE CRILEY, JR.   ARCHITECT

The buildings of this mountain ranch are arranged about an open living area paved with brick. The living room with its high beamed ceiling and wood walls has a large bay window with a low "hikia," from which there is a fine view of the mountains. The raised copper panels above the fireplace are in sharp contrast to the exposed brick surfaces of the chimney.

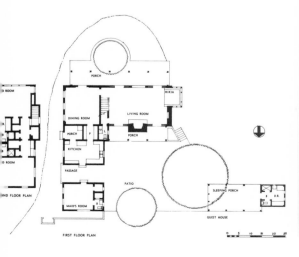

HERBERT STOTHART HOUSE   SANTA MONICA

J. R. DAVIDSON   INTERIOR

96

L. M. MAITLAND HOUSE   LOS ANGELES   J. R. DAVIDSON   INTERIORS

In this library bay is a long built-in couch, with a small book and magazine table at one end. The carpet, couch, walls and ceiling are in shades of warm gray, the draperies a pale coral. The large window areas with Venetian blinds controlling the light, make this a pleasant place for reading. Large sliding doors at one side open upon a covered porch.

High sliding glass doors opening upon a paved terrace afford a magnificent view of the Santa Monica Mountains. The simplicity of the furnishings and the undivided panes of glass create a sense of space and openness. In place of a solid partition between the living room and stair hall, a translucent glass screen is used, through which may be seen a tree begonia. Potted plants are also used as a decorative feature of the stair hall. The patio is sheltered by the house and by garden walls with open wood grilles. A lily pond of geometric form runs along one side of the cement block paving.

J. J. GINSBERG HOUSE · LOS ANGELES

WINCHTON L. RISLEY   ARCHITECT

Making good use of a steeply sloping site, this house is entered at an intermediate landing of the stairs. An interesting vertical accent has been achieved by the use of a glass brick panel placed over the green entry door, affording light to both upper and lower halls. The plan is worthy of study for its compact and convenient arrangement of rooms.

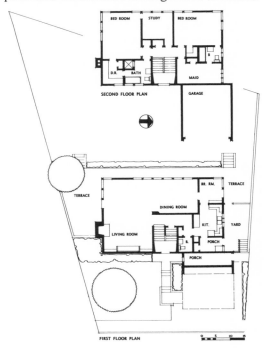

H. N. MILLEA HOUSE   SANTA MONICA   SUMNER SPAULDING   ARCHITECT

This hillside house is subordinated to its setting by the use of natural finished redwood boards. The living room and dining alcove have sliding glass doors which open upon the enclosed, top-screened patio.

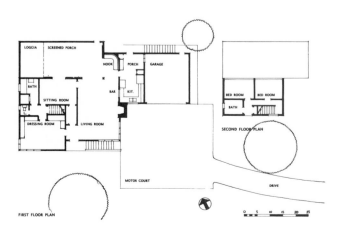

IAN CAMPBELL HOUSE   PASADENA   WEBSTER & WILSON   ARCHITECTS

The treatment of the combined living and
dining rooms shows a careful integration of
design and decoration. Of special interest
is the built-in furniture, which includes a
sofa and end cabinets, a radio unit, a desk,
and book cases. The chief features of the
exterior are the bedroom sun deck and the
wide projecting eaves which protect the
outswinging windows from both rain and
sun. Interior decoration by Honor Easton.

H. C. DAVIDSON HOUSE   PALM SPRINGS

WEBSTER & WILSON   ARCHITECTS

The end of the living room has a curved bank of windows looking out on the desert and mountains beyond. The built-in sofa is of natural redwood and faces both the fireplace and the view. The gay notes of color in the overmantel painting by Martinez are repeated in the upholstery fabrics. Interiors by Honor Easton.

EDWARD KAUFMAN HOUSE   LOS ANGELES   RICHARD J. NEUTRA   ARCHITECT

Unusual in conception, compact and flexible in plan, this house
has been developed through the use of new materials and building methods, free from the restrictions of traditional design.
The exterior is characterized by broad projecting eaves and
continuous bands of windows, with one wall of the stairwell
entirely of glass. The interiors illustrate the use of built-
in furniture and cases to separate the rooms of the first floor.

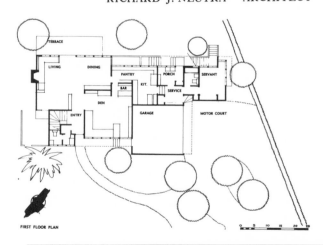

FIRST FLOOR PLAN

MAY WILFLEY HOUSE   LOS ANGELES   ULYSSES F. RIBLE   ARCHITECT

Above: The simplicity of this hall and den and the use of natural finished woods are in complete harmony with the oriental furnishings and decorative details. Interiors by Paul Frankl.

Below: In this balanced composition of curved sofa with attached end tables and lamps, interest is achieved by the use of warm colors and strongly textured materials. From the bay in this game room may be seen the garden and the swimming pool. Interiors by Paul Frankl.

JOE PENNER HOUSE   LELAND F. FULLER

RAYMOND GRIFFITH RANCH HOUSE   CANOGA PARK   LLOYD WRIGHT   ARCHITECT

Against a background of rolling hills this long, low-pitched, rambling house has a very settled and permanent look. In both the exterior and interior striking effects are achieved by the contrast of smooth finished wood and plaster with the rough texture of stonework. The sliding glass doors of the bedrooms open upon an L shaped porch, which is covered by a pergola of interesting design.

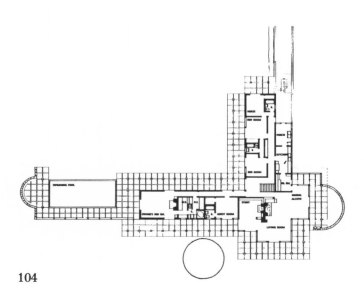

J. J. BUCK HOUSE   LOS ANGELES   R. M. SCHINDLER   ARCHITECT

A conscious attempt has been made to create new and interesting forms, by the massing of windows and plain wall surfaces, and by the use of cantilevered roof projections. The important rooms open upon a lawn area, protected from the street by walls and heavy planting.

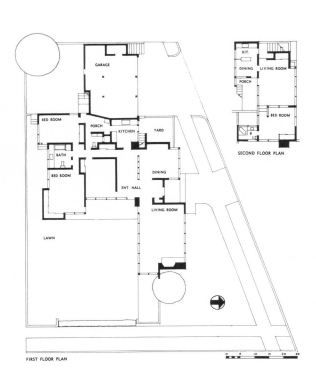

FIRST FLOOR PLAN

ALBERT RUBEN HOUSE   SANTA MONICA   RICHARD J. NEUTRA   ARCHITECT

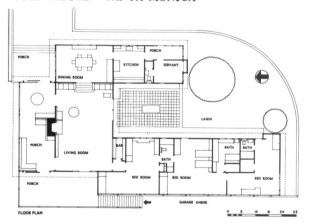

FLOOR PLAN

Impressive in the simplicity of its long unbroken horizontal lines is this house whose lower story is devoted to garages and utility rooms. The rooms of the second story open upon a patio. An important feature is the glazed sun porch, pictured below, which adjoins the living room. Its length is divided by built-in seats and casework in natural finished woods.

H. HARRIS HOUSE   LOS ANGELES

HARWELL HARRIS   INTERIORS

The interior has a repose and simplicity suggestive of the Orient. The walls are almost entirely of sliding and removable doors, glazed with glass and translucent cloth; the floor is covered with grass matting. The lighting is indirect by means of a projecting trough.

Below: The view of the entry hall from the living room shows the use of natural finished plywood paneling extending to door height. The floor is covered with dark linoleum.

G. A. LAING HOUSE   HARWELL HARRIS

T. M. ABELL HOUSE   SANTA MONICA

T. M. ABELL   ARCHITECT

Taking advantage of its hillside location, garden terraces and sun decks have been provided for each of the three floors of this house. The interiors are simple in conception, relying for their interest upon the combination of brick, plaster, and painted wood work as well as the color of the furnishings.

MENSENDIECK HOUSE   PALM SPRINGS

RICHARD J. NEUTRA   ARCHITECT

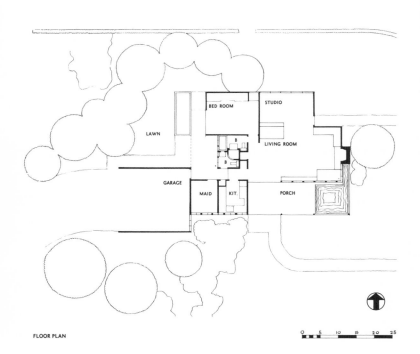

FLOOR PLAN

LAWN   BED ROOM   STUDIO

B   LIVING ROOM

B

GARAGE   MAID   KIT.   PORCH

0   5   10   15   20   25

The strong simple lines of this house, situated on the floor of the desert, are in striking contrast to its rugged background. The plan is flexible in arrangement; the studio may be separated from the living room by a curtain, and sliding doors may be used to close off the screen porch, or all may become one large unit. At the end of the porch is a small reflecting pool, which is lighted by a continuous soffit strip along the outside wall. The planting is admirably suited to the site.